HELP!
I'M A SUBSTITUTE MUSIC TEACHER!

A Collection of Games and Activities for Survival in the Classroom

I0808908

By CHERYL LAVENDER

Basic survival may be your top priority when you accept an assignment as the substitute music teacher! You already know that you face a tightly packed schedule, pages of lesson plans for each grade level and dozens of unfamiliar students eagerly anticipating your every move as their "music sub." By equipping yourself with this kit of time-tested and student-approved songs, games, activities, practice pages and more, you can be assured not only of your own survival (and your students!), but also **success** as their music teacher! You'll find games, large-group activities, small-group cooperative-learning activities and individual projects that are fun and motivating for your students. You won't have to worry about discipline problems when your music students are all actively involved in your music class! Use these substitute plans 1) as complete lessons or 2) as supplements to the regular music teacher's lesson plans. However you choose, be prepared for some invigorating music classes with lots of smiles, participation and, most of all, learning! You and your students never thought music class could be so much fun!

HAL•LEONARD®
CORPORATION
7777 W. BLUEMOUND RD. P.O. BOX 13819 MILWAUKEE, WI 53213

TABLE OF CONTENTS

WARM–UP BODY JIVE

Grade: 1–6

Set–Up: Recording of a favorite song or musical piece with a steady beat

Rationale: Encourage movement to a steady beat; develop sequential movement; develop gross/fine motor skills; develop memory skills

Lesson Sequence: Create either a 4-beat (easy) or an 8-beat (more difficult) series of body motions. For example:

1) Slap legs
2) Clap hands
3) Snap right fingers
4) Snap left fingers

Or add to it:

5) Pat head with both hands
6) Pat shoulders
7) Slap palms of hands together (as if crashing cymbals together)
8) Slap palms of hands together in opposite direction of 7

Lead the students through the series of body motions, counting each motion out loud. When the motions are fluent, call out any number out of sequence and see how quickly they can perform the corresponding motion.

Play the recording of a favorite song or musical piece and perform the body jive to the steady beat of the music. For a challenge, call out a number that is to be omitted (for example, "5"). Continue performing the jive throughout the music, but "rest" on beat 5 instead of patting the head. Gradually, call out additional numbers that are to be omitted, until only one or two motions are left to perform. The tricky part is performing the motions at the proper times by keeping a steady beat! Make sure your students are either counting out loud, or silently "in their heads." Allow a student to lead the activity.

MUSICAL MIRROR MOTIONS

Grade: K-3

Set–Up: Recording of a favorite song or musical piece with a steady beat

Rationale: Encourage movement to a steady beat; develop mirror skills; develop social skills

Lesson Sequence: Pair your students into partners, facing one another. Ask the partners to determine which partner will be the "grasshopper" and which one will be the "caterpillar." Or "pepperoni" and "cheese" could be assigned names. Or use any silly names for fun which your students choose.

Explain that while the music is playing, all grasshoppers will make up a beat motion that the caterpillars will copy at exactly the same time. (For example, clap, slap, tap, pat, march, stomp, sway, bend, jump, etc., are all motions which can be performed to a steady beat.) When your signal is heard (for instance, a tap on the bongo drum), the caterpillars make up a new beat motion and the grasshoppers copy this motion. At each signal, the other partner leads the beat motion.

Variation: Throughout the duration of the recording, allow the grasshoppers to make up a variety of beat motions, with the caterpillars copying. Repeat the activity and switch roles. Play again and pair up new partners.

INSTRUMENTS AROUND THE WORLD

Grade: K–2

Set–Up: Rhythm instruments, one for each student; a recording of a favorite song or musical piece with a steady beat

Rationale: Develop aural perceptual skills; develop identification of classroom instruments; develop rhythm band performance skills; develop social skills; encourage awareness of steady beat

Lesson Sequence: Students are seated in a circle, "around the world." Each student is given an instrument. Explain that while the music is playing the students are to slowly pass the instruments "around the world," from one child to the next, until they hear your signal (perhaps a ring on the triangle). At this point, each student plays a steady beat on the instrument he/she is holding, until your signal is heard. The instruments are passed "around the world" again, until the signal is heard. Continue in this fashion until the end of the music. Play again, and allow a student to give the signal to pass or play.

Variation: When it's time to play instruments, have students play a newly learned rhythm pattern instead of a steady beat. Draw the rhythm on the chalkboard, or place a large card on which the rhythm is drawn in the center of the circle for everyone to see.

MAESTRO'S OBSTACLE COURSE

Grade: K-6

Set–Up: Large grocery-bag mask decorated with a funny face (or a blindfold); four different groups of rhythm instruments (for example, enough drums, maracas, tone blocks and tambourines for approximately half of your group); a conductor's baton

Rationale: Develop focused listening skills; identify instrumental sounds; develop awareness of directionality

Lesson Sequence: Students are standing in a free-formation about the room with space between them, facing you. Show them four different rhythm instruments and explain that the sound produced by each instrument is really a signal for movement in a particular direction. For example, if the tambourine is played, all students are to move with very small footsteps in a forward direction. The sound made by the tone block directs the students to move with very tiny footsteps in a backward direction. The other two instruments indicate movement to the right or left.

Warm–Up: Ask the students to close their eyes (or give each one a blindfold). Play each instrument, one at a time, not in any particular order. While the students are listening to each sound, they are to move in very small movements in the indicated direction until the instrument stops playing. When the sound stops, so do the movements! Giggles and occasional bumps will occur. If students bump into one another, they will not be hurt as they are moving with very small footsteps. Tell them to move away from one another and continue moving in the appropriate direction. When students have moved in many directions lots of times, stop the activity and have them open their eyes. Surprise! Are they standing near the same students as when the activity began? How well did your students' ears tell their feet where to move?

Now, set up **Maestro's Obstacle Course** by selecting a group of students to play in the "band." (With a group of 24, perhaps 12 students could play the four groups of rhythm instruments: three playing tambourines, three playing maracas, etc.). Select one conductor, "Maestro," to lead the band. Select one student to wear the large grocery-bag mask or blindfold. Within the confines of your room, choose a "starting place" and a "goal."

Place the masked student at the starting place, facing the direction of the goal. The remaining students place themselves as "obstacles" between the starting place and the goal in many positions — legs out, arms out, lying on the floor, etc. The positions must be frozen — i.e., the obstacles cannot move.

It is Maestro's job to maneuver the masked student through the obstacle course from the starting place to the goal without bumping into any obstacles! Maestro does this by pointing to a group of band musicians with his/her baton. They play their instruments to indicate the appropriate direction in which the masked student should move in order to reach the goal. (For example, Maestro should point to the tambourines to play if the masked student should move forward.) Maestro must make sure to "cut off" the sounds with a motion of the baton so that players will discontinue playing when the masked student should stop moving in that direction.

When the masked student at last reaches the goal, the number of bumps is tallied. Play again, assigning different students to different roles. See which Maestro can conduct the masked student through the obstacle course with as few bumps as possible!

WOODSTICKS PLAY

Grade: K-3

Set-Up: Pair of woodsticks for each student; recording of a favorite song or musical piece with a steady beat

Rationale: Develop awareness of steady beat; experience rondo form

Lesson Sequence: While the recording of a favorite song or musical piece is playing, instruct students to play woodsticks by tapping them together; tapping them on the floor; alternately tapping on a body part, then together; or any other combination of motions to the steady beat of the music. At your command, "Sunshine," the players stop playing, but feel the steady beat "inside their minds." They may nod their heads or sway their woodsticks to the steady beat. At "Sunshine," the students immediately begin playing their woodsticks to the steady beat. Allow students to be the leaders.

Create a 4-beat or an 8-beat woodstick pattern. For example:

1) Tap the floor
2) Repeat
3) Tap woodsticks together
4) Repeat
5) Tap knees
6) Repeat
7) Tap woodsticks together
8) Repeat

Or with a partner:

1) Tap the floor
2) Repeat
3) Tap both partners' woodsticks
4) Repeat
5) Tap partner's right woodstick with own right woodstick
6) Repeat
7) Tap partner's left woodstick with own left woodstick
8) Repeat

This pattern is called *A.* Students can create another pattern of different motions, called *B,* and yet another pattern of motions, called *C.* While recorded music is playing, perform the entire sequence of patterns in "rondo" form, like this:

A – B – A – C – A

PARTNER SONGS

Grade: 3-6

Set–Up: Music or lyric sheets for these pairs of partner songs:

- "When the Saints Go Marching In" and "Good Night Ladies"
- "He's Got the Whole World in His Hands" and "Go Tell Aunt Rhody"
- "The Farmer in the Dell" and "Here We Go Looby Loo"
- "Merrily We Roll Along" and "London Bridge"
- "She'll Be Comin' Round the Mountain" and "When the Saints Go Marching In"
- "Skip to My Lou" and "Rock-a-My Soul"
- "Here We Go Round the Mulberry Bush" and "Oh Dear, What Can the Matter Be"
- "Three Blind Mice" and "Row, Row, Row Your Boat" and "Are You Sleeping?"

Rationale: Develop vocal harmony skills; develop independent singing skills

Lesson Sequence: Teach or review the partner songs which harmonize together. Begin singing in harmony with your students by having them sing one of the songs together. While they sing, walk around and among them, singing the partner song as you go. Then choose one student to sing and walk about the room with you while both partner songs are sung simultaneously, again. Ask your "companion" student to choose a new student to join your small group. Sing both partner songs again. Ask each of your "companion" students to choose a new student to join your small group. Gradually, your small group of "challenger" students grows, while at the same time the remaining group of students gets smaller. Throughout the activity the entire group develops harmony skills through both listening and singing experiences in a slow-paced, successful and fun manner! Continue adding more students until both singing groups are of equal size.

MUSICAL HULA-HOOPS

Grade: K-2

Set-Up: An assortment of hula-hoops (one hula-hoop to four students); recording of a favorite song or musical piece

Rationale: Develop awareness of spatial limitations; develop social skills; develop awareness of directionality; develop fine and gross motor skill coordination; develop ability to follow directions

Lesson Sequence: Assemble the hula-hoops on the floor around the room, and have four students stand around each hula-hoop. (It's O.K. if a hula-hoop has 2 or 3 students around it instead.) While the music is playing, instruct your students to do one of the following movement activities and continue performing it until your signal (perhaps a jingle on a tambourine) is heard. Insist that all students move in their "own space," and not to move into the space of the student next to or in front of them. Call out a new movement instruction. Continue the activities throughout the duration of the music. Here are some suggested movement activities:

1) Walk, skip, run, jog, hop, jump, gallop, slide, tip-toe, stomp, walk on heels, walk pigeon-toed, walk with toes out, crawl, walk with arms and feet on the floor, walk backwards, fly, swim, row a boat around the hula-hoop.
2) Repeat, but change the direction.
3) Jump into the center of the hula-hoop. Jump back out.
4) Move with one foot inside the hula-hoop and one foot outside.
5) Move with one hand and one foot inside the hula-hoop on the floor and the other hand and foot outside.
6) Move with two hands inside the hula-hoop on the floor and two feet outside.
7) One student goes into the center of the hula-hoop and makes a motion that the others must "mirror" (copy).
8) At your command, "Scatter," all students must go to a new hula-hoop, with the same number of students at each hula-hoop.

See how many more movement ideas you and your students can add to the above list, and play again!

RHYTHM TELEPHONE

Grade: 1-6

Set–Up: Two large blank cards and a marker

Rationale: Develop rhythmic skills through the sense of touch; develop rhythmic dictation skills

Lesson Sequence: Students are seated in a circle, very close to one another, facing counterclockwise. (Students are looking at the back of the next student.) Select a rhythm for the game. For example:

Draw this rhythm on a large card and turn it facedown until the conclusion of the game.

Ask all students to close their eyes and not to open them until you give them a signal (perhaps a ring on the triangle). Tap out the selected rhythm on any student's back by pressing lightly with the fingertips. This student who has just received the rhythm "message" repeats the rhythm by tapping it on the back of the student sitting in front of him/her. The rhythm continues to be passed around the entire circle of students until the last one receives it on his/her back.

At your signal, all students open their eyes. Immediately present the last student to receive the "message" with a large card and marker and ask him/her to write out the rhythm that was tapped on his/her back. Compare this card with the original card and see how the rhythm "message" changed as it was passed around the circle, or if it managed to stay the same! Repeat the game as many times as desired, using new rhythms.

WHO STOLE THE COOKIE FROM THE COOKIE JAR?

Grade: 3–6

Set–Up: None

Rationale: Develop rhythmic speech; develop concentration and memory

Lesson Sequence: All students are seated in a circle. Teach this chant to a few students as a demonstration:

Leader: Who stole the cook – ie from the cook – ie jar?

Leader: Er – i – ca stole the cook – ie from the cook – ie jar!

Erica: Who me?

All: Yeah – you!

Erica: Not me!

All: Then, who?

The chant continues with Erica naming a new student to respond to the questions in the chant. Like this:

Erica: Ja – son stole the cook – ie from the cook – ie jar!

Jason: Who me?

All: Yeah – you! . . . etc.

Next, teach the hand jive:

1) Slap legs
2) Clap hands
3) Snap right fingers
4) Snap left fingers
Repeat.

Conduct the game with all students performing the hand jive until it is established and fluent. Now, all begin saying the chant together, and a designated leader calls out a student's name. The rhythm of the words should fit with the hand jive like this:

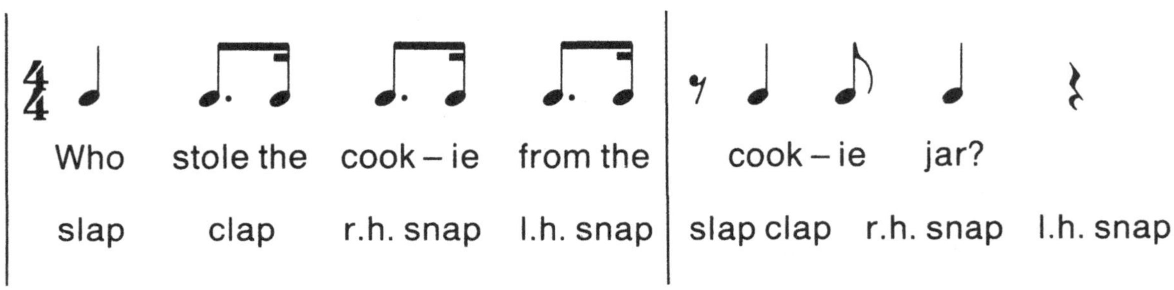

Each student who is called upon must respond to the questions in a firm, clear voice (so everyone in the circle can hear) while performing the hand jive with the rest of the group. If the hand jive rhythm is disrupted, or a student who is responding cannot think of a name to call, he/she sits in the center of the circle and the game continues until only two students are left playing. These two students play until one of them misses the rhythm. The remaining student is the champ.

Options: To create a noncompetitive atmosphere, allow a student who sits in the center of the circle to remain there only until another student misses. Then, he/she can resume a place in the circle and participate as the game continues.

Instead of playing with students' names, assign a number to each student. For example, a leader calls out: "Number 10 stole the cookie from the cookie jar!" Number 10 student responds. If number 10 student misses and takes a turn to sit in the center of the circle, each student remaining in the circle who sits after number 10 must remember that he/she now has a new number. For instance, number 11 is now number 10, number 12 is number 11, and so on!

Change the hand jive to a more complicated pattern. For suggestions, see **Basic Hand and Body Jives**, page 19.

MUSIC CONCENTRATION

Grade: 2-6

Set–Up: None

Rationale: Develop rhythmic speech; develop concentration and memory skills

Lesson Sequence: All students are seated in a circle. Teach this chant:

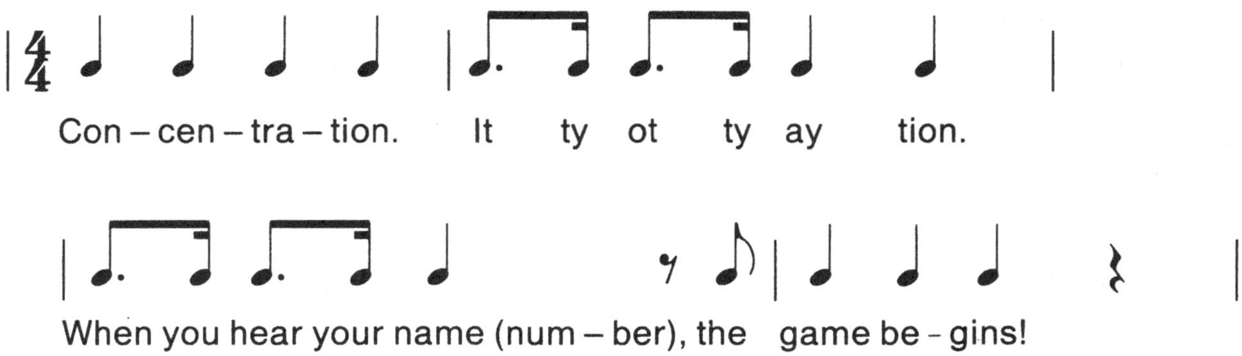

Next, teach the hand jive:

1) Slap legs
2) Repeat
3) Clap hands
4) Repeat

Repeat entire jive throughout the game.

Conduct the game with all students performing the hand jive until it is established and fluent. Now, all begin saying the chant together, and a designated leader calls out his/her own name during the two **slaps** of the hand jive and calls out a new student's name during the two **claps** of the hand jive. The student whose name is called responds by calling out his/her own name during the two slaps of the hand jive and calis out a new student's name during the two claps of the hand jive. This must be done within the rhythm of the hand jive so that the names which are called out are recited in a continuous, uninterrupted flow.

Continue the game until the hand jive becomes disrupted or a student who is responding cannot think of a name to call. A student who "misses" then sits in the center of the circle and the game continues until only two students are left playing. These two students play until one of them misses the rhythm. The remaining student is the champ.

Variations: To create a noncompetitive atmosphere, allow a student who sits in the center of the circle to remain there only until another student misses. Then, he/she can resume a place in the circle and participate as the game continues.

Instead of playing with students' names, assign a number to each student. For example, a student whose assigned number is 10 calls out "10" (during the slaps of the hand jive), and calls out "15" during the claps of the hand jive. Number 15 student responds, and the game continues. If number 15 student misses and takes a turn to sit in the center of the circle, each student who sits after number 15 must remember that he/she now has a new number. For instance, number 16 is now number 15, number 17 is number 16, and so on!

Change the hand jive to a more complicated pattern. For suggestions, see **Basic Hand and Body Jives**, on page 19.

ALPHABET RHYTHMICIANS

Grade: 2-6

Set–Up: 26 slips of paper with a letter of the alphabet printed on each

Rationale: Develop language arts-alliteration skills (same initial word sounds); develop rhythmic speech; encourage verbal improvisation skills

Lesson Sequence: Students are seated in a circle. Give each one a slip of paper on which a letter of the alphabet is printed. (If there are less than 26 students, leave out some letters, starting with the most difficult to form words, such as Q, X, Z, etc. If there are more than 26, simply repeat as many letters on additional slips of paper, as needed.)

Teach this chant (using *A* as an example letter):

A my name is Andy.
My wife's name is Allysa.
We live in Alaska
And we sell Alligators!

Next, teach the hand jive:

1) Slap legs
2) Repeat
3) Clap hands
4) Repeat

Repeat the entire jive throughout the game.

Perform the body jive until it is established and fluent. Then, start with the student who has the letter *A*. He/she recites the chant, substituting the names, place to live and items for sale with words that begin with his/her letter. Continue around the circle. The chant is accompanied with the rhythm of the hand jive. For practice, allow each student an opportunity to practice word substitution while chanting in rhythm.

Now that the game is learned, play again, but do not assign letters. Begin the game as before, starting with a volunteer leader (letter *A*), and continue around the circle. If the hand jive is disrupted, or a student, on his/her turn, cannot think of a substitute word, then that student sits in the center of the circle and the next student in the circle must recite the chant using the **same** letter as the previous student. Continue the game, going through the order of letters in the alphabet until only two students are left. These two students play until one of them misses. The remaining student is the champ.

Variations: To create a noncompetitive atmosphere, allow a student who sits in the center of the circle to remain there only until another student misses. Then, he/she can resume a place in the circle and participate as the game continues.

Options: Create more complex hand jives for more challenge. For suggestions, see **Basic Hand and Body Jives**, on page 19.

BASIC HAND AND BODY JIVES

Grade: 1-6

Set-Up: None

Rationale: Develop fine and gross motor coordination; develop coordination of speech and movement; encourage awareness of steady beat; develop social skills

Lesson Sequence: Once spoken chants or simple songs become familiar, teach your students any of these "jives." They are rhythmic, body percussion accompaniments which are performed with a partner or with the entire class sitting very close together in a circle. Some are easy, some are hard. Some work well for $\frac{2}{4}$, $\frac{3}{4}$, $\frac{4}{4}$, or $\frac{6}{8}$ meter. **All** jives are adaptable to your known songs and chants! Have your students partner-up and create some new jives of their own to share with the class!

Partner Jive in $\frac{3}{4}$:

1) Partners face each other. One partner stretches out hands toward other partner, with one hand at eye level (palm down), the other hand at hip level (palm up). The other partner mirrors this image, so both partners' right and left hands are touching. Slap hands together in this position.
2) Clap partner's hands straight out in front (palms facing toward partner).
3) Clap own hands.

Repeat.

Partner Jive in $\frac{3}{4}$:

1) Clap own hands.
2) Partners clap right hands together.
3) Partners clap left hands together.

Repeat.

Partner Jive in $\frac{6}{8}$:

1) Slap own legs.
2) Tap own shoulders.
3) Clap own hands.
4) Partners clap each other's right hands together.
5) Partners clap each other's left hands together.
6) Partners clap both hands together.

Repeat.

Partner Jive in $\frac{4}{4}$:

1) Slap own legs.
2) Clap own hands.
3) Partners clap each other's right hands together.
4) Clap own hands.
5) Partners clap each other's left hands together.
6) Clap own hands.
7) Partners clap both hands together.
8) Clap own hands.

Repeat.

Partner Jive in $\frac{4}{4}$:

1) Partners clap each other's right hands together.
2) Clap own hands.
3) Partners clap each other's left hands together.
4) Clap own hands.
5) Partners clap both hands together.
6) Clap own hands.
7) Cross own arms and tap shoulders.
8) Slap own legs.

Repeat.

Partner Jive in $\frac{4}{4}$:

1) Partners slap right palms together.
2) Partners slap backs of right hands together.
3) Slap own thigh with right hand.
4) Snap own right fingers.

Repeat.

Whole Class Jive in $\frac{2}{4}$:

1) Students sitting in a circle. Slap own legs.
2) Right hand claps left hand of person sitting to the right, while simultaneously, the left hand claps the right hand of the person sitting to the left.

Repeat.

Whole Class Jive in $\frac{4}{4}$:

1) Students sitting in a circle. Slap own legs.
2) Slap left leg of the person to the right with both hands.
3) Slap own legs.
4) Slap right leg of the person to the left with both hands.

Repeat.

For fun and challenge, use a metronome and increase or decrease the speed (tempo) of the hand/body jive and the chant or song that is being performed.

WALKIE-TALKIE MUSIC FUN

Grade: 1-6

Set-Up: A pair of walkie-talkies (or battery-operated toy telephones); chalkboard or large chart

Rationale: Identify rhythm and/or melody of known songs

Lesson Sequence: Divide students into two teams, A and B. If teams are uneven in number, allow the "extra" student to be score-keeper. Using suggestions from the students, choose familiar songs for use in the game. Draw the song titles on the chalkboard.

Determine starting team. If Team A starts, a student from that team is chosen to be the clue-giver and takes a walkie-talkie outside the room. The other walkie-talkie is given to a member on Team B. The clue-giver outside the room recites this chant into his/her walkie-talkie:

I have a secret song for you.
Can you guess it? Here is a clue!

At this time, he/she taps a phrase of rhythm or hums a phrase of melody from one of the selected songs into the walkie-talkie. The student holding the walkie-talkie inside the room takes one turn to guess the song's title, and speaks it into his/her walkie-talkie. If the answer is correct, then that student trades places with the student in the hall, and the student in the hall resumes a place on Team A. His/her walkie-talkie is given to another team member for answering, and the game continues.

If the student inside the room on Team B answers incorrectly, the walkie-talkie is immediately given to a member on Team A and the secret song clue is repeated. The walkie-talkie continues to be passed from team to team until the correct answer is given. When the correct answer is given, a point is scored for that team.

When all students from both teams have answered, tally the score, or begin the game again, to allow those students who did not have a turn to be clue-givers a chance to answer correctly and take a turn with the walkie-talkie outside the room.

The team with the highest score wins.

RHYTHM DOMINOES

Grade: 2-6

Set–Up: Two pieces of poster board, or construction paper, measuring approximately 6'' x 12'' for each student; one marker for each student; chalkboard; stopwatch

Rationale: Develop rhythmic dictation skills; develop rhythm recognition and identification skills

Lesson Sequence: At the chalkboard, have students take turns drawing rhythm patterns in a selected meter, using combinations of previously learned rhythms. Review the rhythms. These rhythms are the ''pool of rhythms'' from which the dominoes are created.

Instruct each student to divide his/her two poster boards into two sections, as shown. Then, have each student draw a different rhythm (legibly) into each section of one of the two poster boards. Repeat with the other poster board, but have students draw two rhythms that are different from the first poster board. Any rhythm from the chalkboard may be used.

Divide the students into two teams, each forming a circle. Spread the dominoes in the center of each circle, face down. Give the teams an allotted amount of time (for example, two minutes) to overturn the dominoes and create a domino pattern using as many of the dominoes as possible. When the time is up, the team creating the domino pattern using the most dominoes wins.

Collect the poster boards and shuffle. Assemble two new teams, divide the boards between the teams and play again, allotting a shorter completion time. Here is an example of a domino pattern:

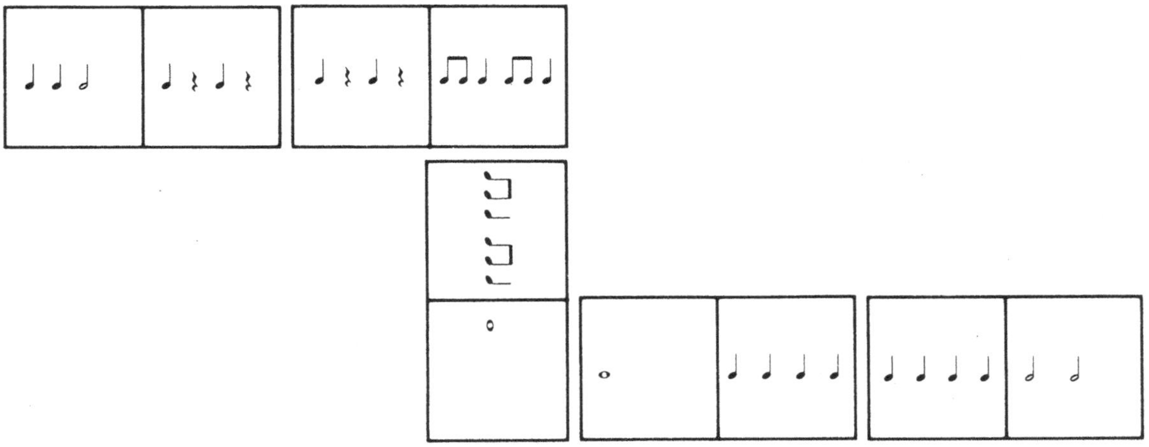

ROCKIN' BODY RHYTHMS

Grade: 2-6

Set–Up: Copies of **Rockin' Body Rhythms** practice page for all students or your own prepared staff sheets with 2, 3, 4 or 5 lines for original compositions

Rationale: Experience staff directionality; develop eye-hand coordination skills; develop gross/fine motor skills

Lesson Sequence: Analyze each line on the staff of **Rockin' Body Rhythms** practice page with your students. (For example, a note on the top line indicates a right-hand snap.) Divide the class into as many groups as there are lines on the staff. Assign a line of the staff to each group. Each group performs the motion indicated by the note on their assigned line at the proper time.

Perform **Rockin' Body Rhythms** again, but exchange parts for more fun and practice.

Now that staff directionality is somewhat familiar, ask all students to perform the entire piece with ALL body motions together. If desired, allow students to create their own versions of body rhythms on your prepared staff sheets of 2, 3, 4 or 5 lines.

ROCKIN' BODY RHYTHMS - 1

ROCKIN' BODY RHYTHMS - 2

SOUNDS AROUND

Grade: 2-6

Set–Up: Paper and pencil for every two students; a stopwatch

Rationale: Develop awareness of musical sounds vs. environmental sounds; develop focused listening skills

Lesson Sequence: Conduct a discussion: What kinds and arrangements of sounds create music? How do these sounds differ from environmental sounds, or "noise"? Pair your students into partners (as private detective teams). Each team is assigned to go out into the school's hallways for a maximum of ten minutes and list on paper every environmental sound that is heard. **The rules:** Hallway conduct must be maintained. Students may come back to the classroom **before** the ten-minute time period is up; if they return **after** the time period is up, the list is disqualified. Teacher should time the investigation with a stopwatch.

When all teams have returned, the lists of sounds are read and described, and the team with the longest list of sounds is the winning team.

Discuss how environmental sounds, or "noise," could be used and arranged in order to create music. How must a composer consider the arrangement of sounds — pitch and duration? Are sounds in music planned or unplanned? What about the use of patterns, rhythms, sequences and special effects such as loud and soft? Draw up a class list which identifies the differences between music and noise.

'PETER AND THE WOLF' – LIVE!

Grade: K–3

Set–Up: Large, unobstructed area for dramatization; recording of "Peter and the Wolf" by Sergei Prokofiev; assorted props and simple homemade masks for each character, such as:

wolf – snout; tail
grandfather – beard; cane
duck – bill; wings
Peter – tunic top; walking stick
cat – whiskers; ears
bird – wings; beak
hunters – hunting hats; tunics or cardboard boot tops

Rationale: Develop aural perceptions of the sounds of instruments of the symphony orchestra; develop creative dramatization skills; develop focused listening skills

Lesson Sequence: If students are not familiar with the music to "Peter and the Wolf," this activity should be conducted in two sessions. During the first session, play the recording while showing pictures of the instruments which portray the various characters in the drama. Instruments included are: the strings, bassoon, flute, clarinet, oboe, French horn and timpani.

In the second session, choose students to play the various characters in the drama of "Peter and the Wolf." Remaining students may "become" the scenery, such as two students sitting with arms outstretched and connected, acting as the "gate"; or many students sitting with hands connected in a circle, acting as the "pond"; or one student standing with arms outstretched acting as the "tree." Assemble the "scenery" about the room, and have the actors in a designated area "offstage."

Play the recording and encourage each actor to move about the "stage area," improvising motions and expressions which typify the character he/she is playing. Each "offstage" student enters the scene when the instrument which plays his/her character's music is heard. For example, when the clarinet is heard, the student who plays the cat enters. This is a favorite activity, and requests of "let's do it again!" are often heard. Allow students to take turns playing different characters for each new dramatization.

MUSICAL SIMON

Grade: K-1

Set–Up: None

Rationale: Develop ability to follow a leader; develop social skills; develop gross and fine motor skills; develop concentration skills

Lesson Sequence: Students stand and face you as the "Musical Simon" leader. Play "Simon Says" in the usual way, except sing a melody on two notes, sol-mi. Suggestions for movement: clap your hands; touch your toes; tap your nose; turn around; slap the ground; jump up high; count to ten; bend your knees; wiggle your fingers; say, "Right on, baby!" Allow students to be the "Musical Simon."

MUSIC VIDEO

Grade: K-4

Set–Up: One medium-size cardboard box; two dowel rods; sheets of lightweight drawing paper and art supplies such as crayons, markers, etc., for each student; transparent tape

Rationale: Develop awareness of how music exists through time; encourage expression of a song's imagery and meaning through the use of art media

Lesson Sequence: Assemble the "music video" cardboard box, as shown, ahead of class time. Allow the students to choose a song as the theme for their music video. Songs that have many verses, or add-on phrases, are good choices, as they offer more possibilities for the video pictorial. Some suggestions: "The Farmer in the Dell," "Old MacDonald Had a Farm," "There Was an Old Woman Who Swallowed a Fly," "Jenny Jenkins," "The Green Grass Grew All Around," "There's a Hole in the Bottom of the Sea," "This Old Man," "She'll Be Comin' Round the Mountain." Allow students to think of more favorites.

Circulate art materials to all students. Assign a different segment or phrase of the song for illustration to each student, so that the music throughout the entire song will be represented on paper. Be sure to assign a page of introduction, which includes the song's title, the name of the music class and date. When each individual picture is complete, assemble all pictures in the correct order from beginning to end, and tape each seam completely with transparent tape so that the pictures form one continuous length of paper. Secure the first picture (the introduction page) to the dowel rod (A) with transparent tape, as shown. Secure the last picture to the other dowel rod (B). Roll up the paper roll onto the second dowel rod (B). Insert the dowel rods into the cardboard box frame so that the introduction page is in view.

Now, all sing the entire song while a student turns the dowel rod (A). The picture representing the words that are being sung is viewed on the "video." This student continues to turn the dowel rod as the students sing, gradually winding up the roll of paper from the dowel rod (B) onto the dowel rod (A). Your students' favorite song comes to life through their own video pictures!

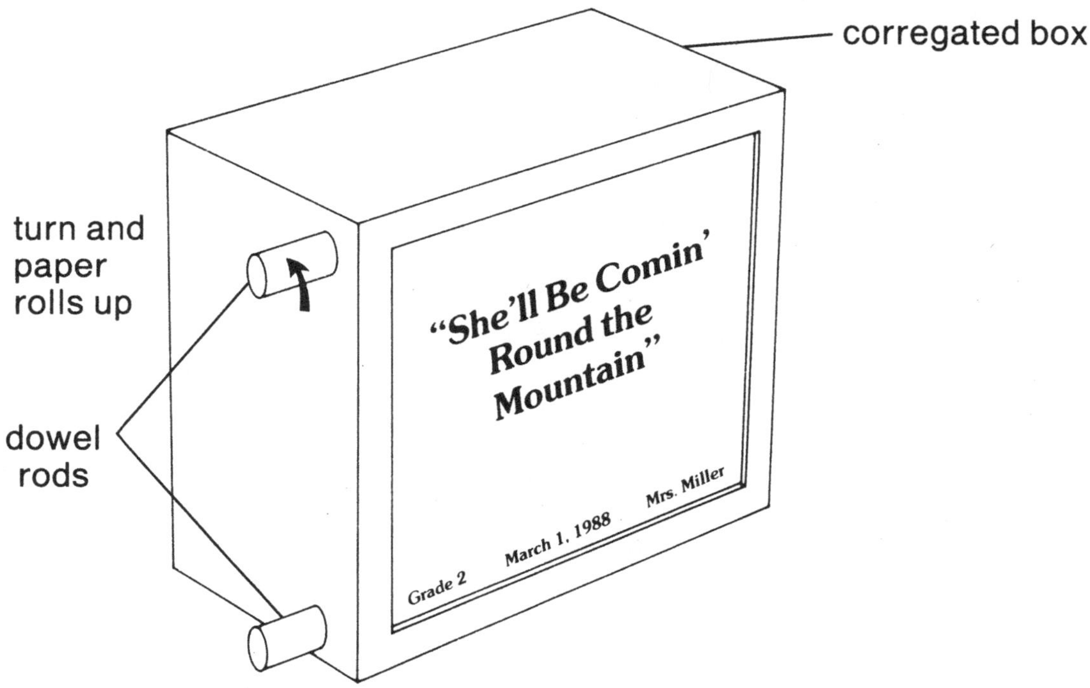

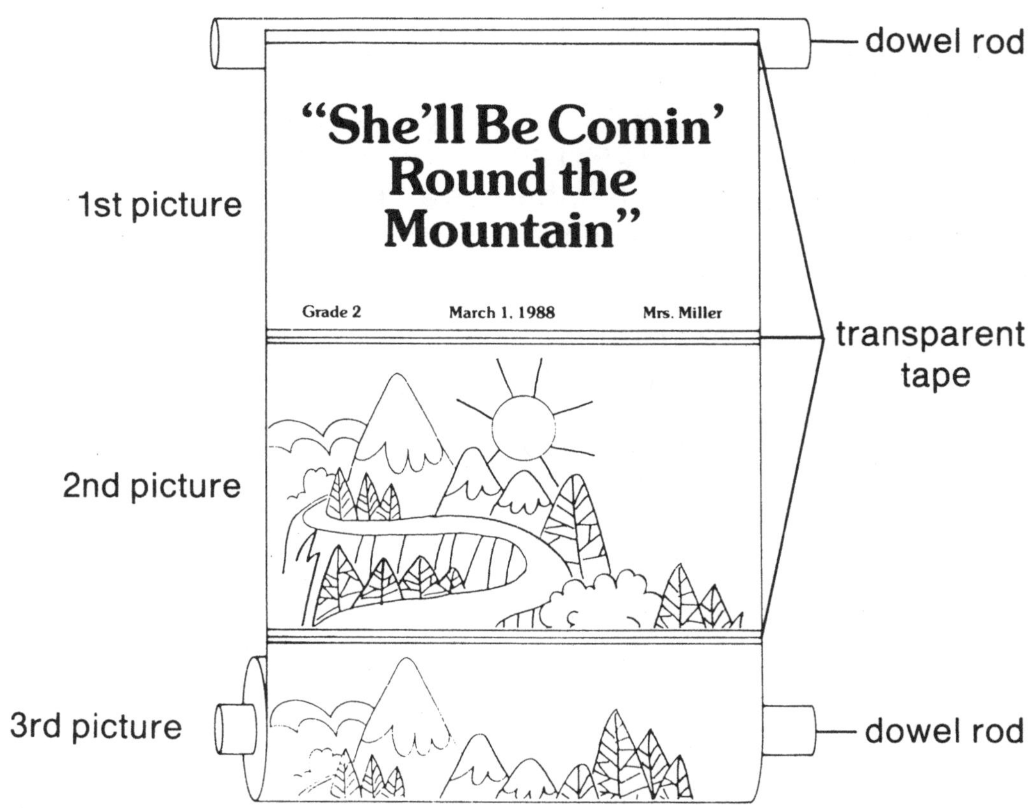

INSTRUMENT OF THE FUTURE

Grade: 2-6

Set–Up: Drawing paper and art supplies, such as crayons, markers, etc., for each student; a recording of "futuristic" sounds produced by a synthesizer

Rationale: Encourage imagination and creativity; develop awareness of "parts relating to the whole"; develop aural perceptions of synthesizer sounds

Lesson Sequence: Initiate a discussion of various musical instruments, such as those of the symphony orchestra, rhythm band, or even homemade instruments. Describe 1) the way each instrument is held, 2) the way it is played, 3) how the sound is produced and 4) the kind of sound that is made.

Explain that a recording of "futuristic" sounds will be played, and that all of the sounds that are heard are produced by an electronic keyboard called a synthesizer. (A synthesizer is not only capable of producing many unusual and original sound effects, but also many of the characteristic sounds produced by ordinary instruments.)

As the sounds are playing, encourage your students to create an original illustration of the "instrument of the future," complete with detailed parts such as valves, slides, mouthpiece, pedals, keys, strings, mallets, and so on. The design of the instrument must be logically thought out, so that there is a "realistic" way for it to be held and played. The different parts of the instrument must work together to form the finished "whole."

When the drawings are complete, allow time for sharing and discussion of each original "instrument of the future." Be prepared for a unique and fun-filled session with some wild imaginations and clever, thought-provoking illustrations!

MUSIC LOOKS LIKE . . .

Grade: K–6

Set–Up: Art materials such as drawing paper, crayons, markers, etc., for each student; recordings of three pieces of music (without words) of contrasting styles, such as "Prelude to the Afternoon of a Fawn" by Claude Debussy, "Prelude #6" from *The Well-Tempered Clavier* by Johann Sebastian Bach, "Fertility of the Earth" from the *Rite of Spring* by Igor Stravinsky

Rationale: Develop awareness of the emotional impact created by contrasting styles of music; encourage expression of feelings and interpretation through art media

Lesson Sequence: Explain that three very different pieces of music will be played. Each has its own unique style and will create special feelings within. Instruct your students to select one crayon or marker to use for the duration of the entire first recording. The object is to draw a continuous line on the paper, without ever letting the crayon/marker leave the paper. Lines may be smooth, jagged, curly, faint, heavy, straight, wavy, etc. When the recording is finished, the crayon or marker may leave the paper. Encourage your students to let the **sounds** of the music move their crayons/markers over the paper! The line should look the way the music sounds!

For the second and third recordings, have your students choose crayons/markers of different colors for use on the same paper. This way, each line representing each style of music is differentiated. When all three recordings are finished, your students have a graphic description of the way each piece of music affected their artistic expression. Allow time for students to share their drawings with one another and describe the similarities and/or differences in style that were perceived while listening to the music.

WANTED: RECORD JACKET DESIGNER

Grade: K-6

Set–Up: Art materials such as sheets of drawing paper, pencils, crayons, markers, etc., for each student; recording of program music, such as "Walk to the Bunkhouse" from *The Red Pony* by Aaron Copland or "Cuckoo in the Deep Woods" from *Carnival of the Animals* by Camille Saint-Saens

Rationale: Develop awareness of how program music stimulates the formation of specific, graphic mental images

Lesson Sequence: Pass out art materials to each student. Explain that the music about to be heard contains sounds which can stimulate the formation of specific, graphic mental images or pictures. Instruct your students to listen intently to the music and to fantasize a story-line that could be depicted by the music, such as the plot to a movie score. From this story-line, encourage your students to use their imaginations and create an original "album jacket" design that illustrates the story-line to the movie. Then have them title it. Share each picture and allow each designer to describe the story-line behind it! For fun, share with your students the original title and story-line of the program music, as well as information about the work and its composer.

INSTRUMENT CHARADES

Grade: 2-6

Set–Up: Recording of sounds of various instruments;* small slips of paper with the name of an instrument (featured on the recording) printed on each

Rationale: Develop instrument identification; develop aural perceptual skills

Lesson Sequence: If your students have seen how instruments are held and played, they'll love this variation on the game charades. Fold the slips of paper and pass them out to your students, IN THE ORDER THE INSTRUMENTS ARE HEARD ON THE RECORDING. As the recording is played, each student, in turn, peeks at the paper he/she is holding. The student who is holding the slip of paper with the instrument that is playing pantomimes as if he/she is playing that instrument. When the sound of the instrument is over, this student may call on others in the class to correctly name the instrument he/she pantomimed. The game may continue until each student has a chance to pantomime an instrument.

* ***Also available:*** *Instrument sound samples CD. This CD contains representative samples of electronic, folk and symphony orchestra instruments, and can be used with* ***Instrument Charades****.*
442-09027 $14.99

INSTRUMENT SLEUTH

Grade: 2-6

Set–Up: Recording of sounds of various instruments;* pictures of those instruments featured on the recording (one instrument for each student)

Rationale: Develop instrument identification; develop aural perceptual skills

Lesson Sequence: Attach a picture of each instrument featured on the recording to the back of each student. The fun part here is that the students can see everyone's instrument except their own! Choose one student to be the "Sleuth." Play through the recording of instrument sounds. While the first instrument is playing, the Sleuth walks among the other students, looking for the student who has the correct instrument on his/her back. The Sleuth then taps that student on the back and the student who is tapped must announce the name of the instrument on his/her own back. This student is now the Sleuth and the game continues until each student has been tapped.

* ***Also available:*** *Instrument sound samples CD. This CD contains representative samples of electronic, folk and symphony orchestra instruments, and can be used with* ***Instrument Sleuth****.*
442-09027 $14.99

INSTRUMENT RELAY

Grade: 2-6

Set–Up: Recording of sounds of various instruments;* pictures of the instruments featured on the recording

Rationale: Develop instrument identification; develop aural perceptual skills

Lesson Sequence: All students are seated in a large circle. Divide them into two teams. Place pictures of each instrument on the floor in front of the players to form an "inner circle." Number the players on each team. Play the recording of instrumental sounds. While a sound sample is playing, player #1 from each team walks among the pictures, searching for the instrument he/she is hearing. When one of the players points to the correct instrument picture, a point is scored for his/her team. Continue with player #2 from each team, and so on, until all the opponents from each team have played. When the last two opponents have played, the round is over and the score is tallied.

* ***Also available:*** *Instrument sound samples CD. This CD contains representative samples of electronic, folk and symphony orchestra instruments, and can be used with* ***Instrument Relay****.*
442-09027 $14.99

POP BOTTLE SYMPHONY

Grade: 2-6

Set–Up: Soda-pop bottles, one per student (all of same size and density); teaspoons, one per student; 2-3 pitchers of water; sticky labels marked Lo-DO, RE, MI, FA, SOL, LA, TI, Hi-DO; copies of "Tunes for Playin'" practice page for each student (or the original practice page projected on a screen with an opaque projector); alcohol wipettes or similar antiseptic preparation for swabbing the mouths of bottles; optional — food coloring

Rationale: Understand the relationship of pitch to the volume or amount of water in a vibrating chamber (when the filled pop bottle is struck with a spoon) and the relationship of pitch to the length of a vibrating air column (when air is blown into the filled pop bottle); understand pitch relationships to one another (more or less water in the same pop bottle produces higher or lower pitch); encourage perception of differences in pitch, from low to high, which make up the Major Scale; develop ensemble playing skills

Lesson Sequence:

1) Playing with Spoons:

a) For every set of eight soda-pop bottles, apply a sticky label to identify each bottle as either Lo-DO, RE, MI, FA, SOL, LA, TI, or Hi-DO. (If your class consists of 24 students, you will have a total of three sets of eight labeled bottles.) Arrange all the Lo-DO bottles together, RE bottles together, etc. Fill the Lo-DO bottles almost to the top with equal amounts of water, so that when struck with a spoon they produce the same low pitch. Next, fill the RE bottles with slightly less water, so that the pitch produced when struck with a spoon sounds RE in the Major Scale and sounds higher than DO. (You may have to play the Lo-DO bottle, then the RE bottle, and/or play the Major Scale on the piano to determine when the water level is correct.) Next, fill the other bottles to complete the Major Scale. Notice that the Hi-DO bottles have the least amount of water; therefore, the vibrating bottle with the least water volume produces the highest pitch and the bottle with the most water volume produces the lowest pitch when struck with a spoon. Play all the bottles in a row through the Major Scale – DO, RE, MI, FA, SOL, LA, TI, DO, and adjust any inconsistencies in pitch by adding or pouring out water.

b) If desired, mix food colors and add a different color to each separately labeled bottle of the Major Scale to visually differentiate the various pitches. For example, all Lo-DO bottles have blue water, all RE bottles have green water, and so on.

c) Distribute soda-pop bottles and spoons to students. Play this little warm-up game. Call out the pitches of the Major Scale from Lo-DO to Hi-DO, one at a time, and ask the students to tap their corresponding bottles. Discuss what happens to the direction of sound as the bottles are played, from those with the most water to those with the least water. Now, call out the pitches in reverse order, so that the Major Scale sounds backwards. Call out pitches in random order to keep students "on their toes."

d) Students may practice playing the melodies from the "Tunes for Playin'" practice page by playing their own bottles when their pitch is to sound in the music. If necessary, for younger students, sing a phrase of pitches from a tune and ask them to echo-sing them back to you. Then, in the same rhythm, have the students play the same phrase of pitches until the entire tune is familiar. Play it through without stopping.

2) Blowing Air into the Bottles: Repeat steps "a" and "b" above.

a) Wipe the mouths of each bottle with an alcohol wipette or similar antiseptic preparation to assure germ-free contact with the bottle. Pass out filled pop bottles to your students.

b) Follow the same directions as in step "c" above, but have your students blow a small stream of air gently across the top of the mouth of the bottle. (It helps to keep the lower lip in contact with the mouth of the bottle, just below the rim.) This takes some practice, as most students want to blow too much air too hard at first. Have them practice forming the word "too" with their lips as they gently blow a small stream of air across the mouth of the bottle, while tipping the bottle slightly away from the upper lip so that the chin comes in contact with the bottle.

c) Follow same directions as in step "d" above.

Variations: Exchange soda-pop bottle with another student and play through the tunes with a new-pitched bottle.

On eight slips of paper, draw Lo-DO through Hi-DO pitches. Fold and put in a box. As each slip is drawn out of the box, one at a time, draw the pitch which is written on it on the chalkboard. Have the students play through this "chance" music.

TUNES FOR PLAYIN'

SCALE FROLIC

THREE BLIND MICE

CHRISTMAS IS COMING

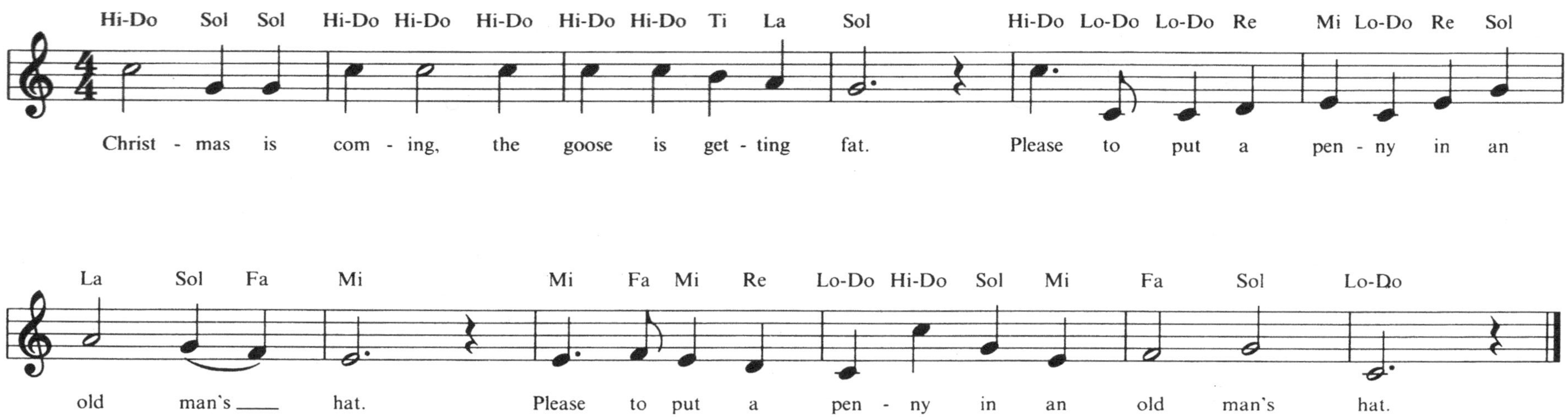

WHITE CORAL BELLS

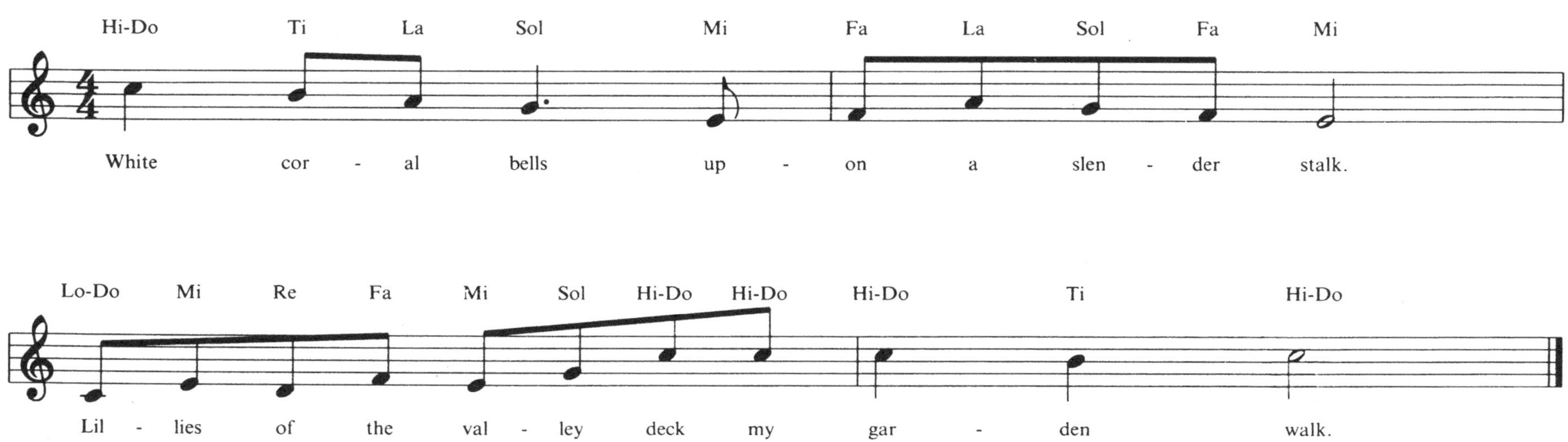

THE MARINE'S HYMN

WEATHER FORECAST: SEVERE THUNDERSTORMS

Grade: 1-6

Set–Up: Proximity to on/off light switch in the classroom

Rationale: Create body percussion sounds which sound like environmental sounds; develop ability to follow visual cues; develop awareness of changes in volume in environmental sounds

Lesson Sequence: All students are seated in a circle. One student operates the on/off light switch, which should be off when the activity starts. As the leader, you will conduct your students through a series of body percussion sounds that mimic the sounds of a real thunderstorm. The storm gradually builds up in intensity, rages, and then gradually subsides. Your **eyes** and **motions** are the only signals that your students will pay attention to as you conduct them to change to a new body percussion sound.

Rules: Students continue performing the same sound until they get a visual cue from you that it's time to change to a new sound.

1) Begin snapping your fingers SLOWLY, alternating right and left hands (not in any particular rhythm, as the sound of raindrops), and look intently at a designated student in the circle. He/she begins to SLOWLY snap his/her fingers like you. Continue snapping and look at the next student; this new student begins to SLOWLY snap his/her fingers while the first student continues snapping. Continue to gaze at each student in turn around the circle until all are snapping like you.

2) As you begin to visually cue for the second sound, all students continue snapping. Change the speed of the snaps to a MEDIUM FAST speed and visually cue the designated student to do likewise. Cue each student in turn around the circle to do the same. Remember, a student does not change the snaps to a MEDIUM FAST speed until he/she gets the visual cue from you to do so.

3) Visually cue each student in turn around the circle to change the speed of the snaps to a FAST speed, beginning with the same designated student.

4) Begin slapping your thighs alternately right and left SLOWLY (not in any particular rhythm, like heavy raindrops falling), and visually cue each student in turn around the circle to do the same.

5) Slap your thighs at a MEDIUM FAST speed and cue students in turn.

6) Slap your thighs at a FAST speed and cue students in turn.

7) Visually cue a small group of students to stomp their feet (like thunder) while the rest of the students continue the sounds of #6. When the feet are stomping, visually cue the student at the light switch to turn the lights on (like lightning). When you cue the stomping to stop, the lights should be turned off. Start and stop the stomping and lights many times to simulate thunder and lightning.

At this point, the storm is raging. When it's time to subside, visually conduct the entire activity in reverse, and the storm will dissolve into the sounds of a few pitter-pattering raindrops.

For fun, tape record the entire activity and play it back. Experience a real thunderstorm right within your classroom without puddles and soggy tennis shoes!